HOPE FOR THE ELEPHANTS

FIRST EDITION
Series Editor Deborah Lock; **Editor** Pomona Zaheer; **Art Editors** Hoa Luc and Yamini Panwar;
DTP Designers Anita Yadav, Vijay Kandwal; **Senior Editor** Linda Esposito;
US Senior Editor Shannon Beatty; **Senior Producer, Pre-Production** Ben Marcus;
Picture Researcher Aditya Katyal; **Illustrator** Hoa Luc; **Managing Editor** Soma B. Chowdhury;
Managing Art Editor Ahlawat Gunjan; **Reading Consultant** Linda Gambrell, PhD;
Subject Consultant Matthew Lewis

THIS EDITION
Editorial Management by Oriel Square
Produced for DK by WonderLab Group LLC
Jennifer Emmett, Erica Green, Kate Hale, *Founders*

Editors Grace Hill Smith, Libby Romero, Michaela Weglinski;
Photography Editors Kelley Miller, Annette Kiesow, Nicole DiMella; **Managing Editor** Rachel Houghton;
Designers Project Design Company; **Researcher** Michelle Harris; **Copy Editor** Lori Merritt;
Indexer Connie Binder; **Proofreader** Larry Shea; **Reading Specialist** Dr. Jennifer Albro;
Curriculum Specialist Elaine Larson

Published in the United States by DK Publishing
1745 Broadway, 20th Floor, New York, NY 10019

Copyright © 2023 Dorling Kindersley Limited
DK, a Division of Penguin Random House LLC
23 24 25 26 27 10 9 8 7 6 5 4 3 2 1
001–333468–Apr/2023

All rights reserved.
Without limiting the rights under the copyright reserved
bove, no part of this publication may be reproduced, stored
in or introduced into a retrieval system, or transmitted, in any
form, or by any means (electronic, mechanical, photocopying,
recording, or otherwise), without the prior written permission
of the copyright owner.
Published in Great Britain by Dorling Kindersley Limited

A catalog record for this book
is available from the Library of Congress.
HC ISBN: 978-0-7440-6839-9
PB ISBN: 978-0-7440-6840-5

DK books are available at special discounts when purchased
in bulk for sales promotions, premiums, fundraising, or
educational use. For details, contact: DK Publishing Special Markets,
1745 Broadway, 20th Floor, New York, NY 10019
SpecialSales@dk.com

Printed and bound in China

The publisher would like to thank the following for their kind permission to reproduce their images:
a=above; c=center; b=below; l=left; r=right; t=top; b/g=background
Dreamstime.com: Altaoosthuizen 7cr, Feathercollector 8clb, Evgeniy Fesenko 7tl, Jostein Hauge 17cra;
Shutterstock.com: APChanel 25tr, Anton_Belov 22cla, BlueOrange Studio 28c, Volodymyr Burdiak 28-29b, Petra Christen 13tr,
DarAnna 12cla, Four Oaks 18tl, Gil.K 26-27b, 29tr, 36-37, Jannarong 31b, Vladislav T. Jirousek 25crb, Don Mammoser 11tr,
Daniel Prudek 31tr, Soranome 44tl, Jen Watson 13cr
Cover images: *Front:* **Shutterstock.com:** Steve Lagreca; *Back:* **Shutterstock.com:** Alfmaler cla, Olzas cra, Tartila cl
All other images © Dorling Kindersley

For the curious
www.dk.com

Level 4

HOPE FOR THE ELEPHANTS

Patricia J. Murphy

CONTENTS

- **6** Introduction
- **8** First Stop: Asia
- **10** Settling In
- **14** How Are Elephants and Humans Alike?
- **18** History of Elephants
- **20** Elephants as Gods
- **24** Elephant Trunk Tricks
- **26** Next Stop: Africa
- **28** Learning About Elephants

36	A Day in the Life of a Savanna Elephant
38	Protecting the Elephants
40	Big Babies Gallery
42	Why Do Elephants Matter?
45	Spread the Hope
46	Glossary
47	Index
48	Quiz

INTRODUCTION

My name is David. I like to collect facts about elephants. My love for these animals began when my Grandma Jo gave me a toy elephant, which I named Babar. My grandma works at a museum. She's creating an exhibit on the future of elephants. She's worried about them. I am, too.

Baby Babar
The name of Babar, a fictional elephant, partly came from the French word for baby (bébé).

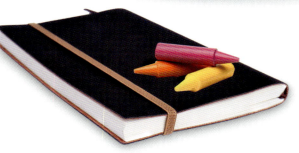

Grandma is traveling to Asia and Africa to study the problems elephants are facing. She invited me along as her helper. We updated our passports, booked our flights, and started packing. I packed my notebook so that I can write about my trip.

Fiction and Fact
In the story, Babar is orphaned when his mother is killed. Today, African and Asian elephants still face dangers in the wild.

7

Teardrop of India
Located off the southeastern coast of India, the island nation of Sri Lanka is nicknamed the "teardrop of India" for its teardrop shape.

FIRST STOP: ASIA

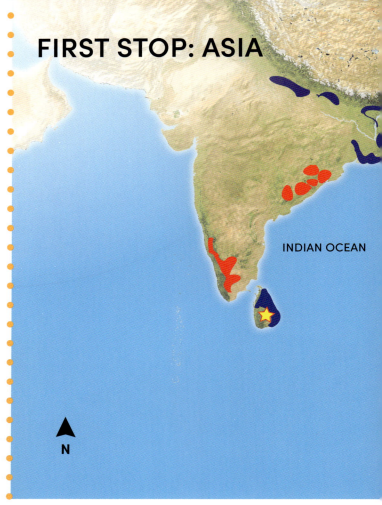

INDIAN OCEAN

N

A Wide Variety
Sri Lanka is home to a large variety of animals.

This map shows where populations of wild Asian elephants can be found. They used to live in many more places and in much larger numbers.

PACIFIC OCEAN

This elephant sanctuary in Sri Lanka is one of many sanctuaries in Asia. Here, tame elephants are cared for in a large, enclosed natural habitat where they can live safely.

Other main populations of wild elephants live in forests across Southeast Asia. Some of these areas have become national parks or reserves where the elephants can be protected.

It's estimated that more than half of the total world population of wild Asian elephants (about 30,000) live in India, including a large population in southwest India. These elephants roam freely.

Changing Habitat
The Sri Lankan elephant was once found throughout Sri Lanka. But as people have developed land, the Sri Lankan elephant has moved to the country's drier regions.

SETTLING IN

We flew for nearly 17 hours and then rode on a bus for six more hours to the elephant sanctuary in Sri Lanka. Stella, the owner, greeted us at the front gates and gave us a tour of the place.

Date: February 21st

We also learned the three sanctuary rules:

1. EVERYTHING is about the elephants. We are here to serve them. They are here to be happy!

2. NO shouting, crowding, or approaching the elephants. They will come to you!

3. LISTEN to the mahouts (the elephant handlers) at all times!

Easy Does It
The mahouts, or elephant handlers, use slow, calm, and steady movements.

11

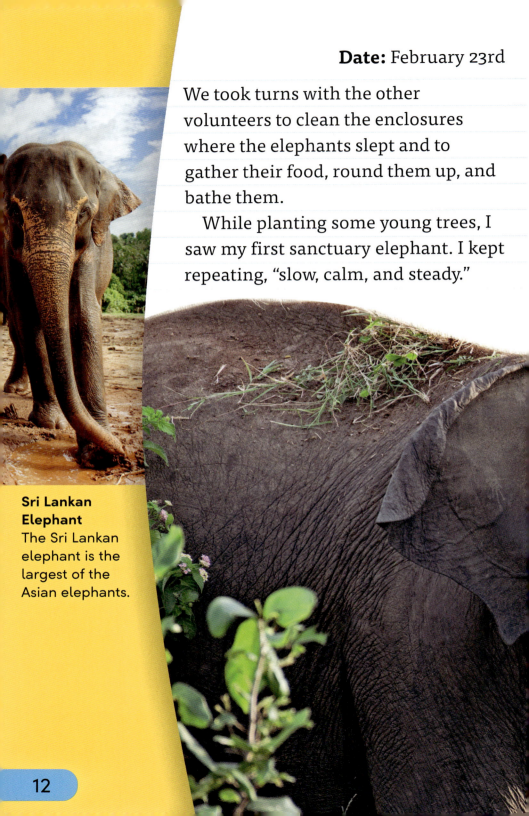

Date: February 23rd

We took turns with the other volunteers to clean the enclosures where the elephants slept and to gather their food, round them up, and bathe them.

While planting some young trees, I saw my first sanctuary elephant. I kept repeating, "slow, calm, and steady."

Sri Lankan Elephant
The Sri Lankan elephant is the largest of the Asian elephants.

It came close, reached out its trunk, and oozed something all over me. *(It was elephant snot!)* I didn't mind. I stared into its soft brown eyes. I can't imagine anyone wanting to hurt these wonderful creatures!

Trunk Talk
Elephants use their trunk to touch and "talk" to other members of the herd.

The tip of the Asian elephant's trunk has one "finger"; an African elephant's has two.

HOW ARE ELEPHANTS AND HUMANS ALIKE?

Here are a few of the similarities between elephants and humans.

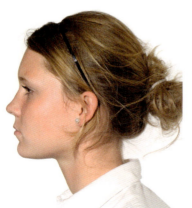  

Memory
We both can have very long memories.

Emotion
We both show a range of emotions, including smiling and crying.

Communication
We both use gestures, such as those for greeting and comforting.

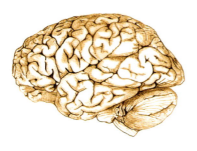

Intelligence
We both behave and act cleverly and learn from our experiences.

Life Span
We both have long lives. Elephants can live to around 70 years old.

15

On the Move
Herds migrate to find food and water.

At daybreak, we joined Stella while she met with the local villagers to ask for their help with the elephants. Afterward, under the hot sun, we walked the elephants to the river. The mahouts made sure they stayed together and didn't stray outside the grounds of the sanctuary.

Date: February 25th

Stella hopes to secure more land for the elephants. She hopes they will return to the wild someday. But in the wild, they'd face the same dangers that wild Asian elephants do. They'd have smaller areas in which to roam, have to compete for food, and might be captured for work or killed by poachers.

Protected
Sri Lankan elephants are protected under a national law. It is illegal to poach, or steal, these animals.

HISTORY OF ELEPHANTS

For 4,000 years, Asian elephants have been an important part of life for people in Asia. People have captured, reared, and trained them for specific purposes. These wild animals lost their freedom.

On the Battlefield
Elephants have been used by armies for transportation and to scare away the enemy.

Religious Ceremony
Elephants continue to be decorated in cloth, bells, and necklaces for festival processions. They carry people and their relics.

Travel and Exploration
In the 19th century, jungle explorers rode elephants and used them to carry their equipment.

Entertainment
Elephants have been and continue to be trained as circus performers. Some countries have now banned this.

Forest Work
Elephants are used for logging work because of their strength.

Tourism
Even today, elephant rides are popular with tourists, especially for trips into the jungle on safaris to look for tigers.

ELEPHANTS AS GODS

The size and power of elephants have inspired people to respect and worship these creatures as gods.

African Elephant Fables
In West African countries, such as Ghana and Cameroon, the elephant in fables represents a wise chief settling arguments in the forest. This headdress is worn for tribal ceremonies.

Airavata
As the king of the Hindu gods, Lord Indra is shown flying Airavata, a magnificent white elephant.

Ganesha

In Hindu tradition, this very popular elephant-headed god helps people achieve success by taking away their problems.

Heavyweight
The Sri Lankan elephant weighs up to 6 tons (5.4 t).

Water Trackers
Elephants can remember the location of a watering hole, even one that's 30 miles (50 km) away.

Date: February 26th

On our last day in Asia, Grandma Jo and I spent the whole time with the elephants—walking, eating, and even swimming with them! Did you know that elephants use their trunks as snorkels?

On our way back to the enclosure, we passed a memorial covered with fresh flowers. Stella explained that this memorial honors elephants they could not—and cannot—save.

Grandma Jo and I took a minute to remember all the people trying to save the elephants.

So Sweet
The Sri Lankan elephant is calm, gentle, and friendly. It has lived alongside people for centuries.

ELEPHANT TRUNK TRICKS

An elephant's trunk is its nose. Besides smelling and breathing, here are some other things an elephant can do with its trunk.

In Charge
Touch its head to show who is in charge or show care for its young.

Wrestling
Wrestle with another bull (male) elephant to show its strength and gain a mate.

Water
Stretch and reach for water to wash and spray itself.

24

Carrying
Curl its trunk for carrying things.

Cleaning
Delicately remove grit, sand, or soil out of its eyes.

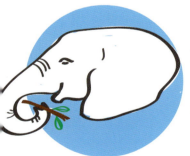

Eating
Grip things for eating.

Rest
Rest on its ivory tusks when it is tired.

Going Green
Elephants are herbivores. That means they eat grasses and leaves. They also use their strong trunks to dig for roots and to pull off tree bark and tree branches.

Built-In Snorkel
An elephant's snorkel-like trunk allows the animal to cross deeper bodies of water.

25

forest elephant

NEXT STOP: AFRICA

Once African elephants were found across most of Africa. There may have been as many as 3 to 5 million of them. Today, the number of elephants has fallen due to poachers hunting for trophies and tusks, smaller areas for roaming, and elephant groups being split up.

This wildlife reserve in Kenya is one of many protected areas for African elephants in the wild.

The forest elephant is found in the tropical rainforest zone of western and central Africa.

savanna elephant

The savanna elephant lives in eastern and southern Africa.

These are small and scattered African elephant populations.

26

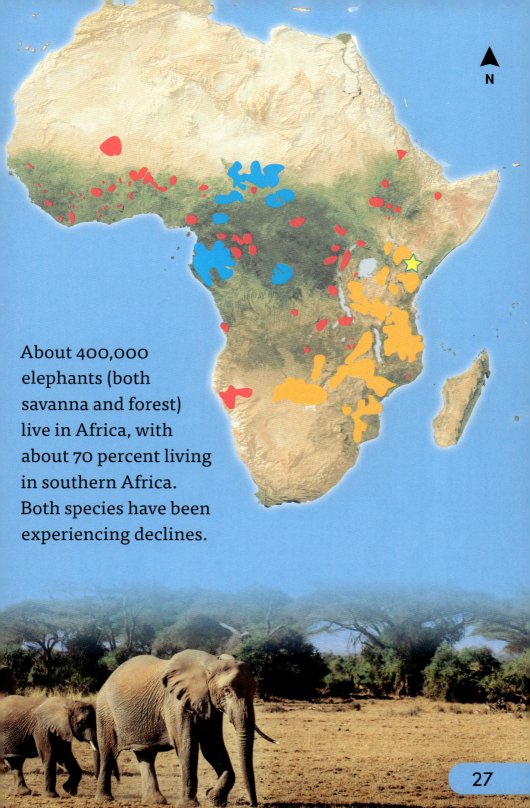

About 400,000 elephants (both savanna and forest) live in Africa, with about 70 percent living in southern Africa. Both species have been experiencing declines.

LEARNING ABOUT ELEPHANTS

After our seven-hour flight to Kenya and a short, bumpy drive, we arrived at the nature reserve.

Related, But Bigger
African elephants are bigger than Asian elephants. African elephants are the world's largest land animal.

Date: February 27th

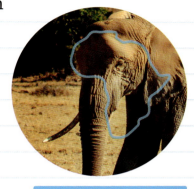

The first people we met were members of the reserve's anti-poaching patrol. We learned that African elephants are poached for their ivory tusks! The reserve is working all day and night to change this. Grandma Jo and I tried to fight back tears when we heard the stories, but we couldn't.

Earth's Largest Ears
An African elephant's ears are shaped like the continent of Africa.

We learned that African elephants are also losing their habitats and their lives, competing with humans for land and food.

Too Spicy
When an elephant smells chili peppers, it might shake its head back and forth, raise its ears, and blow air from its trunk.

Sense of Smell
An elephant's sense of smell is up to 200 times better than a human's.

30

Date: February 27th

Some of the reserve staff are teaching the local villagers ways to prevent elephants from raiding their crops or trampling their farmland.

Some solutions include building fences, growing chili peppers, and hanging beehives on trees. Elephants will stay away from all three of these things.

A Bee Alarm
Elephants make a certain call to warn their herd that bees are nearby.

Today we joined the busy researchers tracking the reserve's elephants to find out about their movements and behaviors and how they could be protected. Some researchers tag the elephants with special collars. This helps them record where the elephants roam.

Naming Elephants
Researchers can identify hundreds of elephants on one reserve. They may use the shapes and characteristics of the elephants' ears to identify each animal.

Einstein or Dolly?
Researchers often use the names of famous musicians, scientists, or artists to remember and identify elephants in a reserve.

Date: February 28th

Others study their dung to find out what the elephants eat! They also record their sounds. Elephants make loud trumpeting and low rumbling sounds, which are lower than we can hear. They make these noises to stay connected with their family nearby and far away.

Tagging
Researchers work quickly to tag an elephant. They give the animal a shot that puts it briefly to sleep. The researchers make sure that the animal stays healthy throughout the short tagging process.

Elephant being tagged with an electronic device

Snares
Snares are wire strands strung low to the ground. Elephants and other animals don't see them and can become easily entrapped.

Suddenly, word came that an elephant was trapped in a snare! The de-snaring team and mobile veterinary unit raced to save it. First, they calmed the elephant with a sleeping drug.

Then, they removed the wire snare before cleaning and stitching the elephant's wounds. Soon the elephant was as good as new and could return to the wild—but there's still the danger of this happening again. Snares are everywhere!

Calves Caught
Young elephants, or calves, have an especially hard time breaking free from the snares. The wires also cause more damage to their growing bodies.

A DAY IN THE LIFE OF A SAVANNA ELEPHANT

From dawn to dusk, elephants roam the African savanna, searching for and eating large amounts of food.

1:00 pm—Bath
Elephants cool down from the midday heat.

11:00 am—Shower
A dust shower helps keep the insects away.

6:00 am—Food
An elephant digs in the soil for salt. Salt is an important part of its diet.

6:00 pm—More Food
A branch, or even a whole tree, makes a tasty evening meal.

10:00 pm—Water
Elephants take an evening stroll to the water hole for another drink of water.

37

A Family Affair
Females in a herd take care of each other's calves.

Date: March 1st

PROTECTING THE ELEPHANTS

Today, we visited the reserve's orphan nursery! We met a girl named Daphne. Her father works as one of the nursery's elephant keepers. The keepers act as the orphans' family members. Most of the orphans lost their mothers to poachers in the African savanna.

An orphan needs a lot of love, care, and special milk to stay alive.

When these babies grow up, they'll join the reserve's wild elephants.

Daphne and I fed one orphan, Edwin, a bottle. Grandma Jo and I sang him to sleep with an Irish lullaby. It was the same one Grandma Jo used to sing to me!

Mother's Milk
Calves can drink as much as 3 gallons (11 l) of their mother's milk a day.

Creature Comforts
Elephant babies suck their trunk, much like a human baby sucks their thumb.

BIG BABIES GALLERY

From the moment elephants are born, they are a big part of the family. They are cared for by their mothers, aunts, and other members of the herd. Their survival depends on this.

A Big Welcome
Hello, world! I'll be up on my feet soon.

Healthy Drinks
I get tired and thirsty following my mom around all day. Luckily, she's always close by for a drink.

Endless Playtime
A piggyback ride at bath time is so much fun! There's a good view from here. Whoops, I'm slipping!

Plenty of Snuggles
The best place to snuggle and rest is curled up right next to my mom!

Family Reunions
Spending time with my whole herd is the best time of all. One day, I'll be as big as my mom!

WHY DO ELEPHANTS MATTER?

Elephants are the largest land animals. Plants and other animals depend upon them in many ways.

Hefty Appetite
Elephants can eat up to 600 pounds (272 kg) of food a day.

Seeds
An elephant may deposit an estimated 3,200 seeds a day.

Poop Protection
Elephant poop protects seeds from being eaten by beetles.

Plant Dispersal and Growth

1. Elephants eat huge amounts of plants.

2. Some plant matter is pooped out and forms new plants. Other animals then eat these plants.

3. Some plant seeds need to go through the digestive system of elephants to be able to start growing.

Fresh Water
Elephants dig wells with their tusks, providing many places for fresh water.

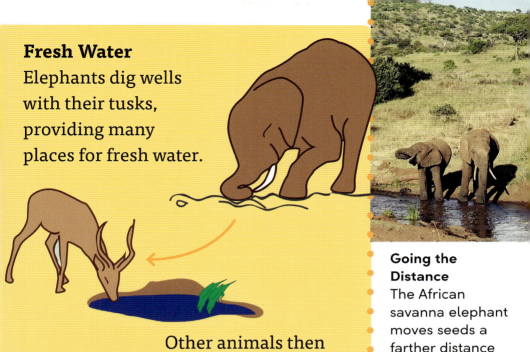

Other animals then use these wells.

Going the Distance
The African savanna elephant moves seeds a farther distance than any other savanna land animal.

Forest Growth
Elephants make trails across a large area. As they move around, they knock down large plants.

Smaller plants are then able to grow in the sunlight.

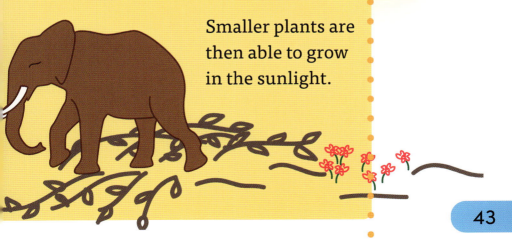

Happy Birthday! When a calf is born, the females in a herd trumpet to announce its arrival.

Date: March 2nd

On our final day of the trip, Daphne handed me a picture she drew with the word "TUMAINI," which means "hope." She told us that it's now our job to spread the word—and be the hope for the elephants!

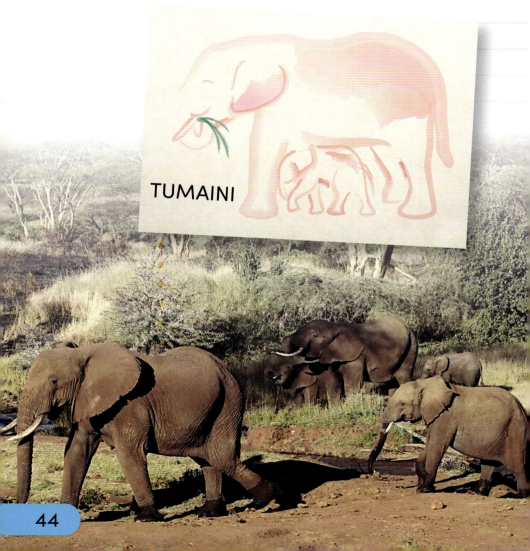

SPREAD THE HOPE

You can be the hope for elephants, too.

 Don't buy anything made of ivory or that looks like ivory, and tell your family and friends not to buy them either.

 Don't buy products that harm elephants' natural habitats. Instead, choose paper and wood products with the Forest Stewardship Council (FSC) sign.

 Don't visit places where elephants are forced to perform tricks or work hard.

 Do visit national parks, or reserves and sanctuaries, that promote elephant-friendly tourism and jobs for villagers.

 Do sponsor an orphaned elephant at a sanctuary or raise money for the World Wildlife Fund or other organizations that help save and protect elephants.

Ecotourism
Ecotourism is one way that people who share their land with elephants can both make money and save these animals. Elephant-friendly tours allow visitors to see elephants in their natural habitats. They can enjoy elephants just being elephants. There are no rides or tricks.

45

GLOSSARY

Ecotourism
Trips to watch wildlife without harming their habitats

Exhibit
A display of objects

Mahout
Someone who trains and handles elephants

Mobile veterinary unit
Vets traveling around in a vehicle containing medical equipment for helping animals

Orphan
An animal whose parents have died

Poaching
Killing and stealing animals without permission

Reserve
A protected area set aside for animals

Sanctuary
A place of safety

Savanna
Large area of flat grassland with few trees found in hot countries

Snare
Trap for capturing animals

Volunteer
Someone who does a job without getting paid

INDEX

African elephants 26–37
  compared to Asian elephants 13, 28
  dangers to 26, 29, 30, 34–35
  ears 29
  fables 20
  map 27
  population 26, 27
Asian elephants 8–23
  compared to African elephants 13, 28
  dangers to 17
  habitat 10
  history 18–19
  map 8–9
  sanctuaries 9, 10–13, 16–17
  size 12, 22
Babar 6, 7
baby elephants (calves)
  birth announcement 44
  caught in snares 35
  drinking 39, 40
  herd's care for 38, 40, 41
  orphans 38–39
  playing 41
battlefield elephants 18
bee alarm 31
calves *see* baby elephants (calves)
circus performers 19
communication
  bee alarm 31
  birth of calf 44
  like humans 14
  sounds 33
  trunk "talk" 13

dangers to elephants
  habitat loss 26, 30
  poachers 17, 26, 29, 38
  snares 34–35
dung (poop) 33, 42
ears 29
ecotourism 45
elephant sanctuaries 9, 10–13, 16–17
emotion 14
food 25, 36, 37, 42
forest elephants 26
gods, elephants as 20–21
herbivores 25
herds 16, 38
Hindu gods 20–21
history of elephants 18–19
hope for elephants 45
humans
  history with Asian elephants 18–19
  similarities to elephants 14–15
importance of elephants 42–43
India 9
intelligence 15
ivory 29, 45
Kenya wildlife reserve 26, 28–33, 38–39
life span 15
mahouts (elephant handlers) 11, 16
maps
  Africa 27
  Asia 8–9
memory 14, 22
migration 16
naming elephants 32
orphans 38–39

plant dispersal and growth 42, 43
poachers 17, 26, 29, 38
poop (dung) 33, 42
religion 18, 20–21
savanna elephants 26, 36–37, 43
sense of smell 30
snares 34–35
Sri Lanka
  elephant protection law 17
  elephant sanctuary 9, 10–13, 16–17
  location 8
Sri Lankan elephant 10, 12, 22
tagging elephants 32, 33
tourism 19, 45
tracking elephants 32
trunks
  baby elephants 39
  "finger" 13
  as snorkels 22, 25
  touching and "talking" 13
  tricks 24–25
tusks 29, 43
water holes 22, 37
working elephants 18–19

47

QUIZ

Answer the questions to see what you have learned. Check your answers in the key below.

1. In which country does more than half of the wild Asian elephant population live?
2. What is an elephant handler called?
3. What is the name of the Hindu elephant-headed god?
4. True or False: An elephant's trunk is only used for smelling.
5. How do researchers track the movements of elephants in the reserve?
6. Why do elephants dig in the dirt?
7. Which part of an elephant's body do researchers look at to identify each animal?
8. Name three solutions that the reserve staff offered to keep elephants out of villagers' farmland.

1. India 2. A mahout 3. Ganesha 4. False 5. They place a tag with an electronic device on their collar 6. To get salt 7. The elephants' ears 8. Building fences, growing chili peppers, and hanging beehives on trees